HAL•LEONARD INSTRUMENTAL PLAY-ALONG

TROMBONE

Great Themes

T0086594

HOW TO USE THE CD ACCOMPANIMENT:

A MELODY CUE APPEARS ON THE RIGHT CHANNEL ONLY. IF YOUR CD PLAYER HAS A BALANCE ADJUSTMENT, YOU CAN ADJUST THE VOLUME OF THE MELODY BY TURNING DOWN THE RIGHT CHANNEL.

THE CD IS PLAYABLE ON ANY CD PLAYER, AND IS ALSO ENHANCED SO MAC AND PC USERS CAN ADJUST THE RECORDING TO ANY TEMPO WITHOUT CHANGING THE PITCH.

ISBN 978-1-4234-9199-6

HAL•LEONARD® CORPORATION

7777 W. BLUEMOUND RD. P.O. BOX 13819 MILWAUKEE, WI 53213

Visit Hal Leonard Online at
www.halleonard.com

CONTENTS

◆ AXEL F

Theme from the Paramount Motion Picture BEVERLY HILLS COP

TROMBONE

By HAROLD FALTERMEYER

Fine

mf

D.S. al Fine
(with repeats)

❷ BELLA'S LULLABY
from the Summit Entertainment film TWILIGHT

TROMBONE

Composed by
CARTER BURWELL

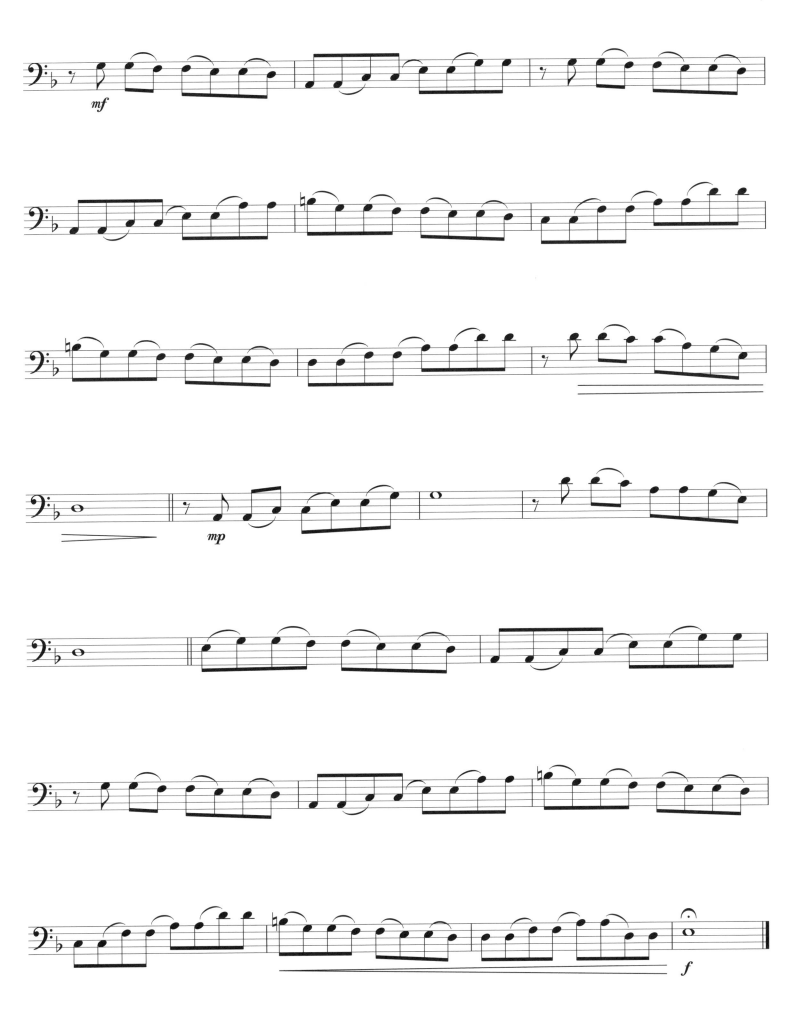

❸ BONANZA
Theme from the TV Series

TROMBONE

Words and Music by
JAY LIVINGSTON and RAY EVANS

◆ 4 BUGLER'S DREAM (OLYMPIC FANFARE)

TROMBONE

By LEO ARNAUD

◆ CHARIOTS OF FIRE

from CHARIOTS OF FIRE

TROMBONE

Music by VANGELIS

◆ GET SMART

from the Television Series

TROMBONE

By IRVING SZATHMARY

❼ HAWAII FIVE-O THEME

from the Television Series

TROMBONE

By MORT STEVENS

❽ I LOVE LUCY
from the Television Series

Lyric by HAROLD ADAMSON
Music by ELIOT DANIEL

TROMBONE

❾ THE MEDALLION CALLS

from Walt Disney Pictures' PIRATES OF THE CARIBBEAN: THE CURSE OF THE BLACK PEARL

TROMBONE

Music by KLAUS BADELT

❖ NEWHART MAIN TITLE THEME

from the TV Series NEWHART

TROMBONE

By Henry Mancini

THE ODD COUPLE

Theme from the Paramount Television Series THE ODD COUPLE

TROMBONE

By NEAL HEFTI

ROMEO AND JULIET (LOVE THEME)

from the Paramount Picture ROMEO AND JULIET

By NINO ROTA

TROMBONE

13 LOVE THEME FROM "ST. ELMO'S FIRE"

from the Motion Picture ST. ELMO'S FIRE

TROMBONE

Words and Music by
DAVID FOSTER

◆ SPANISH FLEA

TROMBONE

Words and Music by
JULIUS WECHTER

15 THEME FROM "SCHINDLER'S LIST"

from the Universal Motion Picture SCHINDLER'S LIST

TROMBONE

Music by JOHN WILLIAMS

HAL•LEONARD INSTRUMENTAL PLAY-ALONG

Your favorite songs are arranged just for solo instrumentalists with this outstanding series.
Each book includes a great full-accompaniment play-along CD so you can sound just like a pro!
Check out **www.halleonard.com** to see all the titles available.

Disney Greats

Arabian Nights • Hawaiian Roller Coaster Ride • It's a Small World • Look Through My Eyes • Yo Ho (A Pirate's Life for Me) • and more.

_____ 00841934	Flute	$12.95
_____ 00841935	Clarinet	$12.95
_____ 00841936	Alto Sax	$12.95
_____ 00841937	Tenor Sax	$12.95
_____ 00841938	Trumpet	$12.95
_____ 00841939	Horn	$12.95
_____ 00841940	Trombone	$12.95
_____ 00841941	Violin	$12.95
_____ 00841942	Viola	$12.95
_____ 00841943	Cello	$12.95
_____ 00842078	Oboe	$12.95

Glee

And I Am Telling You I'm Not Going • Defying Gravity • Don't Stop Believin' • Keep Holding On • Lean on Me • No Air • Sweet Caroline • True Colors • and more.

_____ 00842479	Flute	$12.99
_____ 00842480	Clarinet	$12.99
_____ 00842481	Alto Sax	$12.99
_____ 00842482	Tenor Sax	$12.99
_____ 00842483	Trumpet	$12.99
_____ 00842484	Horn	$12.99
_____ 00842485	Trombone	$12.99
_____ 00842486	Violin	$12.99
_____ 00842487	Viola	$12.99
_____ 00842488	Cello	$12.99

Movie Music

And All That Jazz • Come What May • I Am a Man of Constant Sorrow • I Walk the Line • Seasons of Love • Theme from Spider Man • and more.

_____ 00842089	Flute	$10.95
_____ 00842090	Clarinet	$10.95
_____ 00842091	Alto Sax	$10.95
_____ 00842092	Tenor Sax	$10.95
_____ 00842093	Trumpet	$10.95
_____ 00842094	Horn	$10.95
_____ 00842095	Trombone	$10.95
_____ 00842096	Violin	$10.95
_____ 00842097	Viola	$10.95
_____ 00842098	Cello	$10.95

Elvis Presley

All Shook Up • Blue Suede Shoes • Can't Help Falling in Love • Don't Be Cruel • Hound Dog • Jailhouse Rock • Love Me Tender • Return to Sender • and more.

_____ 00842363	Flute	$12.99
_____ 00842367	Trumpet	$12.99
_____ 00842368	Horn	$12.99
_____ 00842369	Trombone	$12.99
_____ 00842370	Violin	$12.99
_____ 00842371	Viola	$12.99
_____ 00842372	Cello	$12.99

Sports Rock

Another One Bites the Dust • Centerfold • Crazy Train • Get Down Tonight • Let's Get It Started • Shout • The Way You Move • and more.

_____ 00842326	Flute	$12.99
_____ 00842327	Clarinet	$12.99
_____ 00842328	Alto Sax	$12.99
_____ 00842329	Tenor Sax	$12.99
_____ 00842330	Trumpet	$12.99
_____ 00842331	Horn	$12.99
_____ 00842332	Trombone	$12.99
_____ 00842333	Violin	$12.99
_____ 00842334	Viola	$12.99
_____ 00842335	Cello	$12.99

TV Favorites

The Addams Family Theme • The Brady Bunch • Green Acres Theme • Happy Days • Johnny's Theme • Linus and Lucy • NFL on Fox Theme • Theme from the Simpsons • and more.

_____ 00842079	Flute	$10.95
_____ 00842080	Clarinet	$10.95
_____ 00842081	Alto Sax	$10.95
_____ 00842082	Tenor Sax	$10.95
_____ 00842083	Trumpet	$10.95
_____ 00842084	Horn	$10.95
_____ 00842085	Trombone	$10.95
_____ 00842086	Violin	$10.95
_____ 00842087	Viola	$10.95
_____ 00842088	Cello	$10.95

Twilight

Bella's Lullaby • Decode • Eyes on Fire • Full Moon • Go All the Way (Into the Twilight) • Leave Out All the Rest • Spotlight (Twilight Remix) • Supermassive Black Hole • Tremble for My Beloved.

_____ 00842406	Flute	$12.99
_____ 00842407	Clarinet	$12.99
_____ 00842408	Alto Sax	$12.99
_____ 00842409	Tenor Sax	$12.99
_____ 00842410	Trumpet	$12.99
_____ 00842411	Horn	$12.99
_____ 00842412	Trombone	$12.99
_____ 00842413	Violin	$12.99
_____ 00842414	Viola	$12.99
_____ 00842415	Cello	$12.99

Twilight – New Moon

Almost a Kiss • Dreamcatcher • Edward Leaves • I Need You • Memories of Edward • New Moon • Possibility • Roslyn • Satellite Heart • and more.

_____ 00842458	Flute	$12.99
_____ 00842459	Clarinet	$12.99
_____ 00842460	Alto Sax	$12.99
_____ 00842461	Tenor Sax	$12.99
_____ 00842462	Trumpet	$12.99
_____ 00842463	Horn	$12.99
_____ 00842464	Trombone	$12.99
_____ 00842465	Violin	$12.99
_____ 00842466	Viola	$12.99
_____ 00842467	Cello	$12.99

Wicked

As Long As You're Mine • Dancing Through Life • Defying Gravity • For Good • I'm Not That Girl • Popular • The Wizard and I • and more.

_____ 00842236	Book/CD Pack	$11.95
_____ 00842237	Book/CD Pack	$11.95
_____ 00842238	Alto Saxophone	$11.95
_____ 00842239	Tenor Saxophone	$11.95
_____ 00842240	Trumpet	$11.95
_____ 00842241	Horn	$11.95
_____ 00842242	Trombone	$11.95
_____ 00842243	Violin	$11.95
_____ 00842244	Viola	$11.95
_____ 00842245	Cello	$11.95

FOR MORE INFORMATION, SEE YOUR LOCAL MUSIC DEALER, OR WRITE TO:

HAL•LEONARD® CORPORATION

7777 W. BLUEMOUND RD. P.O. BOX 13819 MILWAUKEE, WI 53213

ARTIST TRANSCRIPTIONS®

Artist Transcriptions are authentic, note-for-note transcriptions of today's hottest artists in jazz, pop and rock. These outstanding, accurate arrangements are in an easy-to-read format which includes all essential lines. Artist Transcriptions can be used to perform, sequence or for reference.

CLARINET

00672423	Buddy De Franco Collection	$19.95

FLUTE

00672379	Eric Dolphy Collection	$19.95
00672372	James Moody Collection – Sax and Flute	$19.95
00660108	James Newton – Improvising Flute	$14.95

GUITAR & BASS

00660113	The Guitar Style of George Benson	$14.95
00699072	Guitar Book of Pierre Bensusan	$29.95
00672331	Ron Carter – Acoustic Bass	$16.95
00672307	Stanley Clarke Collection	$19.95
00660115	Al Di Meola – Friday Night in San Francisco	$14.95
00604043	Al Di Meola – Music, Words, Pictures	$14.95
00673245	Jazz Style of Tal Farlow	$19.95
00672359	Bela Fleck and the Flecktones	$18.95
00699389	Jim Hall – Jazz Guitar Environments	$19.95
00699306	Jim Hall – Exploring Jazz Guitar	$19.95
00604049	Allan Holdsworth – Reaching for the Uncommon Chord	$14.95
00699215	Leo Kottke – Eight Songs	$14.95
00675536	Wes Montgomery – Guitar Transcriptions	$17.95
00672353	Joe Pass Collection	$18.95
00673216	John Patitucci	$16.95
00027083	Django Reinhardt Antholog	$14.95
00026711	Genius of Django Reinhardt	$10.95
00672374	Johnny Smith Guitar Solos	$17.99
00672320	Mark Whitfield	$19.95

PIANO & KEYBOARD

00672338	Monty Alexander Collection	$19.95
00672487	Monty Alexander Plays Standards	$19.95
00672520	Count Basie Collection	$19.95
00672364	Warren Bernhardt Collection	$19.95
00672439	Cyrus Chestnut Collection	$19.95
00673242	Billy Childs Collection	$19.95
00672300	Chick Corea – Paint the World	$12.95
00672537	Bill Evans at Town Hall	$16.95
00672548	The Mastery of Bill Evans	$12.95
00672425	Bill Evans – Piano Interpretations	$19.95
00672365	Bill Evans – Piano Standards	$19.95
00672510	Bill Evans Trio – Vol. 1: 1959-1961	$24.95
00672511	Bill Evans Trio – Vol. 2: 1962-1965	$24.95
00672512	Bill Evans Trio – Vol. 3: 1968-1974	$24.95
00672513	Bill Evans Trio – Vol. 4: 1979-1980	$24.95
00672381	Tommy Flanagan Collection	$24.99
00672492	Benny Goodman Collection	$16.95
00672486	Vince Guaraldi Collection	$19.95
00672419	Herbie Hancock Collection	$19.95
00672438	Hampton Hawes	$19.95
00672322	Ahmad Jamal Collection	$22.95

00672564	Best of Jeff Lorber	$17.99
00672476	Brad Mehldau Collection	$19.99
00672388	Best of Thelonious Monk	$19.95
00672389	Thelonious Monk Collection	$19.95
00672390	Thelonious Monk Plays Jazz Standards – Volume 1	$19.95
00672391	Thelonious Monk Plays Jazz Standards – Volume 2	$19.95
00672433	Jelly Roll Morton – The Piano Rolls	$12.95
00672553	Charlie Parker for Piano	$19.95
00672542	Oscar Peterson – Jazz Piano Solos	$16.95
00672544	Oscar Peterson – Originals	$9.95
00672532	Oscar Peterson – Plays Broadway	$19.95
00672531	Oscar Peterson – Plays Duke Ellington	$19.95
00672563	Oscar Peterson – A Royal Wedding Suite	$19.99
00672533	Oscar Peterson – Trios	$24.95
00672543	Oscar Peterson Trio – Canadiana Suite	$10.99
00672534	Very Best of Oscar Peterson	$22.95
00672371	Bud Powell Classics	$19.95
00672376	Bud Powell Collection	$19.95
00672437	André Previn Collection	$19.95
00672507	Gonzalo Rubalcaba Collection	$19.95
00672303	Horace Silver Collection	$19.95
00672316	Art Tatum Collection	$22.95
00672355	Art Tatum Solo Book	$19.95
00672357	Billy Taylor Collection	$24.95
00673215	McCoy Tyner	$16.95
00672321	Cedar Walton Collection	$19.95
00672519	Kenny Werner Collection	$19.95
00672434	Teddy Wilson Collection	$19.95

SAXOPHONE

00672566	The Mindi Abair Collection	$14.99
00673244	Julian "Cannonball" Adderley Collection	$19.95
00673237	Michael Brecker	$19.95
00672429	Michael Brecker Collection	$19.95
00672315	Benny Carter Plays Standards	$22.95
00672314	Benny Carter Collection	$22.95
00672394	James Carter Collection	$19.95
00672349	John Coltrane Plays Giant Steps	$19.95
00672529	John Coltrane – Giant Steps	$14.99
00672494	John Coltrane – A Love Supreme	$14.95
00672493	John Coltrane Plays "Coltrane Changes"	$19.95
00672453	John Coltrane Plays Standards	$19.95
00673233	John Coltrane Solos	$22.95
00672328	Paul Desmond Collection	$19.95
00672379	Eric Dolphy Collection	$19.95
00672530	Kenny Garrett Collection	$19.95
00699375	Stan Getz	$19.95
00672377	Stan Getz – Bossa Novas	$19.95
00672375	Stan Getz – Standards	$18.95

00673254	Great Tenor Sax Solos	$18.95
00672523	Coleman Hawkins Collection	$19.95
00673252	Joe Henderson – Selections from "Lush Life" & "So Near So Far"	$19.95
00672330	Best of Joe Henderson	$22.95
00672350	Tenor Saxophone Standards	$18.95
00673239	Best of Kenny G	$19.95
00673229	Kenny G – Breathless	$19.95
00672462	Kenny G – Classics in the Key of G	$19.95
00672485	Kenny G – Faith: A Holiday Album	$14.95
00672373	Kenny G – The Moment	$19.95
00672326	Joe Lovano Collection	$19.95
00672498	Jackie McLean Collection	$19.95
00672372	James Moody Collection – Sax and Flute	$19.95
00672416	Frank Morgan Collection	$19.95
00672539	Gerry Mulligan Collection	$19.95
00672352	Charlie Parker Collection	$19.95
00672561	Best of Sonny Rollins	$19.95
00672444	Sonny Rollins Collection	$19.95
00675000	David Sanborn Collection	$17.95
00672528	Bud Shank Collection	$19.95
00672491	New Best of Wayne Shorter	$19.95
00672550	The Sonny Stitt Collection	$19.95
00672350	Tenor Saxophone Standards	$18.95
00672567	The Best of Kim Waters	$17.99
00672524	Lester Young Collection	$19.95

TROMBONE

00672332	J.J. Johnson Collection	$19.95
00672489	Steve Turré Collection	$19.95

TRUMPET

00672557	Herb Alpert Collection	$14.99
00672480	Louis Armstrong Collection	$17.95
00672481	Louis Armstrong Plays Standards	$17.95
00672435	Chet Baker Collection	$19.95
00672556	Best of Chris Botti	$19.95
00673234	Randy Brecker	$17.95
00672448	Miles Davis – Originals, Vol. 1	$19.95
00672451	Miles Davis – Originals, Vol. 2	$19.95
00672450	Miles Davis – Standards, Vol. 1	$19.95
00672449	Miles Davis – Standards, Vol. 2	$19.95
00672479	Dizzy Gillespie Collection	$19.95
00673214	Freddie Hubbard	$14.95
00672382	Tom Harrell – Jazz Trumpet	$19.95
00672363	Jazz Trumpet Solos	$9.95
00672506	Chuck Mangione Collection	$19.95
00672525	Arturo Sandoval – Trumpet Evolution	$19.95